SERVING KOSHER WINE

WITH

TRADITIONAL HOLIDAY MEALS

Best Wishes
Susan Raskin

International Kosher Wine Suggestions

Susan Raskin

SERVING KOSHER WINE

WITH

TRADITIONAL HOLIDAY MEALS

Susan Raskin

"THIS BOOK IS DEDICATED TO EVERYONE WHO
PREPARES TRADITIONAL HOLIDAY MEALS."

CONTENTS

FOREWORD
xi

INTRODUCTION
xv

CHAPTER ONE
A LITTLE HISTORY OF WINE
1

CHAPTER TWO
WINE AND SPIRITUALITY
5

CHAPTER THREE
HOW WINE IS MADE.
HOW IT IS MADE KOSHER
7

CHAPTER FOUR
ISRAELI AND INTERNATIONAL KOSHER
WINE REGIONS AND WINERIES
13

CHAPTER FIVE

SHOPPING FOR KOSHER WINE –
THINGS TO CONSIDER
15

CHAPTER SIX

STORING AND SERVING
WINES AT HOME
19

CHAPTER SEVEN

PAIRING WINE WITH FOOD:
SOME GUIDELINES
23

CHAPTER EIGHT

TRADITIONAL HOLIDAY DISHES
AND WINE STYLES THAT WORK
WELL WITH THEM
27

CHAPTER NINE

YOUR PERSONAL WINE JOURNAL
43

FOREWORD

Who did eat the fat of their sacrifices, And drank the wine of their drink-offering?...Deuteronomy 32:38

Is there anything more rewarding than researching a book? Researching this book on wine and holiday meals involved reminiscing with family members and friends, and it also entailed reading legions of great books and articles on delicious traditional foods and fine wines from around the world. It could hardly get better than this. But then again, I also had to *sample* these scrumptious goodies. I had to sip a smooth, rich Merlot from Israel while sautéing potato latkes. I had to swirl a fragrant, dark, and spicy Shiraz from Australia while slicing a delectably tender brisket. I had to note how the refreshing effervescence of the sweet Italian Moscato contributed wonderfully to the honey drizzled fresh fruit plate. And all these wines were kosher!

My interest in the ever-evolving and always-fascinating subject of wine is not new, and it is not confined to only kosher wines. I enjoy exploring regional wines that are off the beaten path. This interest has led me to sampling local honey wines while visiting tribal villages in Cameroon, Africa. Studying the art of wine made me—and some of my fellow wine club members—scrutinize hundreds of bottle labels and the cartons that they had been shipped in. We discovered countless themes, such as animals, new-age designs, European classical paintings, and philosophical notes from the winemakers and winery owners. We then had a unique opportunity to enjoy some of our wonderful found art—and, of course, to sip the wines—when a local gallery allowed us to exhibit these bottles and cartons all as an installation. A number of kosher bottles were represented.

My introduction to fine wines came about decades ago when I was briefly working at the Fifth Avenue office of Horizon Pictures for the late, great film producer Sam Spiegel (who produced *The African Queen, On The Waterfront, Nicolas and Alexander*, etc.) while he was working on his final film, *Betrayal*. I often took notes while attending the production meetings he held at some of the best restaurants in the city. He always ordered exceptional wines, which I was privileged to sample. Great vintage Rieslings were definitely among his favorites! Another job in Manhattan had me assisting in the planning of a very formal reception for a member of a European royal family; only the best wines from the best vineyards would do.

When I lived in Australia for a few years, I was again blessed with wonderful wine experiences. My good friend Arline says I have a "busted matzah," (her preferred expression for "great luck,") and I agree with her! I had the opportunity to meet the late Len Evans, whom many consider to be the father of the Australian wine scene. His restaurant in the Rocks area of Sydney was *the* place to be to if you wanted to learn about and sample some of the newest and finest wines from the up-and-coming regions Down Under. I recently revisited Australia and it was amazing to see how much the industry had grown. There were very good kosher wines in Australia, as well as neighboring New Zealand.

While wonderful fine wines always accompanied social dinner parties at my young family's home, only the familiar sweet kosher wines ever found a place at the holiday table. My children's dear, late grandfather, Nat, first introduced me to this style of wine. His explanation was that this simple Concord grape wine was the only kosher wine he had ever known, and it was always on his parents',

Harry and Ida's, holiday table. With little knowledge about kosher wines, I opted to carry on his tradition.

Now, after years of professional experience leading hundreds of educational seminars, private and public tastings, and becoming a certified sommelier, I have learned much about wine in general and the ever-widening world of *fine* kosher wine. I am happy to share some of my knowledge with you.

All styles of wine around the world are available in kosher form, and they include wines that are delicious, sophisticated, smooth, dry, sweet, bubbly, organic, and vegan. It is time to add a new element to your traditional holiday meals: wonderful and *fine* kosher wine!

INTRODUCTION

...wine gladens the hearts of man...Psalms 104:15

Wine has been around for thousands of years. At times, people drank wine only during purely ceremonial, spiritual, or religious events, and at other times they drank wine daily as a safe alternative to polluted or unavailable water. Beginning eight thousand years ago in the Mediterranean region, wine can now be found in almost every country on earth. Its modern-day popularity is due in no small part to the advances made in vineyard management and new winemaking techniques. Universities and large wine companies in New Zealand, Australia, South Africa, Argentina, the United States, and other countries have invested a lot of money into the science of creating quality wine.

Kosher wines are experiencing wonderful growth in terms of the areas that are producing them and in their quality levels. The quality of wine has increased so dramatically that many wines receive international acclaim and are awarded very high ratings from prestigious organizations such as the *Wine Spectator*, *Wine Enthusiast*, and *Wine Advocate*. It is now possible to enjoy superb offerings from international kosher winemakers at very affordable prices.

Many people's earliest experiences with kosher wines were centered on family meals, particularly holiday meals. Many a host or hostess has offered an oftentimes very sweet wine accompanied, perhaps, by a long-simmered, tender pot roast or a juicy, flavorful baked chicken with savory herbs served around a backdrop of the laughter and banter of their cousins, grandparents, and old family friends. These gatherings are often cherished for the warm loving feelings and memories that they conjure up.

While we enjoy continuing many holiday culinary traditions, we always have the opportunity to add new elements by including wonderful, quality kosher wines from Israel and around the world. These delicious wines will complement your meals and add to the enjoyment of your special occasion.

L'Chyaim

CHAPTER ONE

A Little History of Wine

"Therefore G-d gave thee of the dew of heaven, and the fatness of
the earth, and plenty of corn and wine."
—Genesis 27:28.

No one knows exactly when and where the very first wines were made. In fact, wild grapes can mix with the naturally occurring yeast on their skin and ferment into a wine without any human involvement at all. What we do know, however, is that civilizations have been enjoying wine for a long, long time. Detailed records of wine production from thousands of years ago have been discovered in the eastern end of the Mediterranean region. It is widely believed that wines were produced from fruits other than grapes in ancient Persia as early as 6000 BCE.

Wine that was made from grapes came a little bit later on—sometime around 3000 BCE in Mesopotamia and Egypt. As early cultures advanced in agriculture and commerce, trade routes developed, which enabled the expansion of wine production and distribution throughout the Mediterranean and into Europe. Inscriptions on ancient jugs, scrolls, artwork, and the written inventories of royal and wealthy households detail everything from the harvesting of the grapes to elaborate feasts and ceremonies that featured wine. Although wine is mostly made from fermented grapes, additives such as salt water, herbs, and spices were often used, and at times the wines were even smoked. Nevertheless, condemnation for some of these practices can be found in ancient poetry (In his *Odes*, the Roman Poet Catullus writes, "Away with you, Water, destruction of wine"), and high praise for ancient wines are found in historical writings and documents, such as author and viticulturalist Pliny the Elder's *Natural History*, 23-79 CE.

AND THEN, ISRAEL

The ancient viticultural history of Israel is strong in large part because of her access to a number of important trade routes, including the ancient Via Maris, the Ridge Route, and King's Highway. There is archaeological evidence for the kinds of grapes that were grown and the wines that were produced and sold in Israel during biblical times. Of course, the spiritual element of wine is deeply embedded in the Jewish lifestyle. The Kiddush (a blessing that is made over the wine) is recited throughout the Hebrew holiday year. The grape was even declared one of the seven blessed species of fruit in the Book of Deuteronomy (8:8). For over two thousand years, Israel had many vineyards. Many of her wines were considered excellent, and they were exported throughout Europe. Unfortunately, during the conquest of Israel in 636 CE, all of Israel's vineyards were destroyed, and the indigenous grape varieties were torn out. After the Crusades, which were around 1300 CE, viticulture was briefly reintroduced, but it didn't fully thrive until the late nineteenth century, when the wealthy Frenchman Baron Edmond De Rothschild of the famous wine family donated a huge sum of money to Israel to advance wine production. This generous gift enabled vineyard owners in Israel to plant several French varietals. Cabernet Sauvignon, Merlot, Cabernet Franc, Chardonnay, Sauvignon Blanc, and others were brought in. Wineries were established and winemakers from France came to instruct locals on then-current wine making techniques. However, by today's standards the quality of the wine wasn't so great. Most wines were made for religious ceremonies; they were not intended to complement a meal or be enjoyed on its own. Nowadays, of course, Israel produces very good wines, both kosher and non-kosher.

Delicious, refreshing, food-friendly, and elegant kosher wines are also being made in many other countries around the world. Some important international areas that produce kosher wine include the United States (California and New York in particular), Argentina (especially the Mendoza region), Australia (especially the famed Margaret River area in western Australia), Austria, Chile, France, Hungary, Italy, Portugal, and Spain.

CHAPTER TWO

Wine and Spirituality

"Blessed art thou, O lord G-d, King of the universe, creator of the fruit of the vine."
—Kiddush

Because wine is mentioned hundreds of times in the Talmud and Old Testament, it is easy to see why it has played an important role in Jewish culture for thousands of years. It is said that Noah planted grape vines immediately after The Flood. This indicates how important it was—and still is—to have wine available for nearly every Jewish ceremony. Along the way, very strict rules were developed for processing grapes into wine to ensure the sanctity of the wine

Wine is a vital component of many Judaic life-cycle events. The weekly Shabbat has its Kiddush to sanctify the day, and is included at the Havdalah. During a brit milah, which is the covenant of circumcision, the infant's lips are coated with wine. During a Bar Mitzvah or Bat Mitzvah, the first blessing may be recited over wine. Additionally, in traditional Jewish weddings the bride and the groom ceremoniously share two glasses of wine. It is a Purim tradition to drink wine. For Passover, four glasses of wine represent the four biblical expressions of redemption G-d promises to the Israelites while they were enslaved. Additionally, the Festival of Shavuot begins with the lighting of candles and a traditional blessing over the wine.

CHAPTER THREE

What is Wine and how is it Made Kosher?

"I shall return my people from captivity, and they shall build up the waste cities and inhabit them and they shall plant vineyards and drink the wine from them."
–Amos 9:14-15

THE GRAPE

You may find alcoholic beverages labeled "wine," even though it is made from fruit other than grapes, but true wine is made from grapes. The highest quality wines are made from the *Vitis Vinifera* species. There are thousands of grapes in this species, but the world's most popular wines, including fine kosher wines, are made from fewer than fifty varieties of grape. These kosher wines include everybody's favorites: Cabernet Sauvignon, Merlot, Malbec, Shiraz (Syrah), Gamay, Chardonnay, Pinot Grigio, Sauvignon Blanc, Viognier, Riesling, etc.

Then there is the *Vitis labrusca* species. One variety in this group, the Concord grape, is found in the northeastern United States. It was this grape that early Jewish immigrants found in abundance and used to create the widely recognized sweet, red kosher wine. Cherished by many for it's traditional inclusion at holiday tables, it is not on par with quality wines made from *Vitis vinifera*.

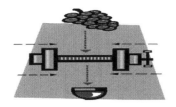

THE WINEMAKING PROCESS

Making good wine requires skill, knowledge, and cooperation from nature. It is a complex process, and when everything works together the result can be truly delicious!

After lying dormant through the winter, grape vines awaken with new growth by budding in the spring. The grapes form just after the flowers appear, and they mature during the spring and summer. Once the winemaker and the vineyard manager feel that the grapes have reached their appropriate ripeness, which they judge in large part by the sugar levels, they pick the grapes either by hand or by machine. The grapes are then transported to the winery, which is located either at the vineyard or elsewhere. Once they are delivered, the grapes usually go through a stemmer and crushing process. This process helps separate stems and skins, and it helps release the juice from the grapes, which allows the sugars in the juice to be exposed to the naturally occurring yeast on the skin of the grape. Oftentimes, additional yeast is added to promote the fermentation process and to add certain desirable nuances to the flavor. Did you know that the juice from over 95 percent of red wine grapes is white? With most rosé wines, the grape skins are left in the juice for a short period—just enough time to allow for a little bit of coloration. To create red wines the dark skins are left in the tank or barrel with the juice to extract even more color. White wines are made by removing the skins before fermentation.

The juice is put in large temperature-controlled containment tanks—which can be stainless steel or cement—where it ferments into wine. Some very high quality wines are made by a process called barrel fermentation, in which the juice is put into oak barrels to derive flavor nuances from the oak during the fermentation process. The costliness of this method is reflected in the price of the wines that are made this way. It takes anywhere from several days to several weeks for the juice to turn into wine. The quality and flavors produced during fermentation are the results of several factors, including temperature of the liquid, the sugar content of the grapes, the nutrients contained in the juice, and other considerations. After the fermentation process is complete, the wine may be filtered or clarified to remove any small floating particles by using egg whites, bentonite (a clay), gelatin, casein (a dairy derivative), or isinglass (from fish). Most kosher wines use bentonite. After the filtering process is complete, the wine can be aged further in barrels or bottles, or it can be bottled and shipped out to our dinner tables. There are, however exceptions to this process. You can find unfiltered wines aged "sur lie," which means that bits of grape and dead yeast cells are left in the wine to add complexity as the wine develops.

WHAT MAKES A WINE KOSHER?

While most kosher designations are commonly made for particular types of food, in winemaking there are many additional considerations. All kosher wines are made under strict rabbinical supervision. The rabbi does not bless the wine, but ensures its sanctity by overseeing its production. All of the people directly involved in the creation of kosher wines following the harvest must be observant Jewish males. The equipment, the storage facilities, and even the barrels must be either new or used exclusively for kosher wines. Any ingredients other than grapes, such as the types of yeast and the fining/filtering materials, all factor into a wine's kosher certification. There are three basic types of kosher wines: Kosher, Kosher for Passover, and Mevushal, which is always Kosher but not necessarily for kosher Passover.

ISRAELI KOSHER WINE

Kosher wines made in Israel (not all Israeli wines are kosher) have seven requirements that must be adhered to all under strict rabbinical supervision:

1. After planting a vine, winemakers must wait four years to harvest the grapes.

2. No other fruit or vegetable can be grown in between the rows of vines.

3. All of the winemaking supplies must be kosher. Additionally, no animal products can be used in the winemaking process. Instead of egg whites, gelatin, casein, or isinglass, a clay material called Bentonite is generally used to clarify the wine.

4. The winemaking equipment and the location where the wine is stored must be kosher as well, and they must maintain very high standards of cleanliness.

5. All people who are directly involved in the hands-on process after harvesting the grapes must be Sabbath-observing Jews. A non-observant winemaker can give instructions, but he cannot touch the wine.

6. Just over 1 percent of the wine produced must be ceremoniously poured away in recognition of the days of the Jerusalem Temple.

7. In Israel, after the fourth year of harvesting, the vines must lie idle every seventh year.

KOSHER WINES MADE OUTSIDE OF ISRAEL

As in Israel, all of the winemaking supplies must be kosher, of course, when kosher wines are made outside of Israel. All people involved in the hands-on processes after the grapes have been harvested must be Sabbath-observant Jews. All of the equipment and storage facilities must be kosher. Everything must occur under strict rabbinical supervision.

MEVUSHAL (an important type of kosher wine)

Mevushal can be translated as, "boiled wine." Why is this process necessary? Ancient customs required that kosher wine be boiled. Boiling the wine rendered it unfit for enjoyment by idol-worshipping non-Jews, which ensured its sanctity status. Making the wine unappealing in this manner preserved the sanctity— although not always the flavor—of the wine in situations where non-Jews handled it. Thankfully, a modern process called flash pasteurization is now used to produce Mevushal wines. The wine is quickly heated to 185 degrees Fahrenheit, and then it is quickly cooled. This process may compromise the flavor and aging potential of some of these wines, but one can nonetheless find many wonderful Mevushal wines. A study at the University of California at Davis suggests that little flavor difference exists between flash-pasteurized and unpasteurized wines. Catering companies around the world generally use Mevushal wines when kosher wines are required. If you have non-Jewish guests at your kosher table, it is a good option to have a Mevushal wine available. With Mevushal wines there are no concerns about preserving the kosher status of the wine. The label on the bottle will either say "Mevushal" or "M," and it will also contain a kosher symbol. A few examples of kosher symbols you might see on wine bottles can be found in Chapter Five.

KOSHER FOR PASSOVER

Along with the myriad requirements for general kosher certification, Kosher for Passover wine has additional ones. Among these include: they can only be made with yeasts that has not been grown on bread. They also can't contain common preservatives like potassium sorbate or additives that are in sweet kosher wines, such as corn syrup. The bottles for these wines will state "Kosher for Passover" on the label and Mevushal (if it is.)

Note: There are many, many—and again, many—symbols used for various kosher designations. Remember to check the labels! It is important to look for the appropriate symbols on the wine bottles to determine kosher status. "K," "P," "U," or any of dozens of other symbols may be present on the label to indicate its kosher status.

CHAPTER FOUR

Israeli and International Kosher Wine Regions

*"And behold this vine…was planted in a good soil by great waters
that it may bring forth branches and that it may bear fruit, that it
might be a goodly vine."*
–Ezekiel 17:7

There are five major grape-growing regions in Israel:

1. <u>GALILEE:</u> Widely acknowledged as Israel's highest quality wine-producing area, Galilee has a number of microclimates, including Lower Galilee, Upper Galilee, and Tabor. Wonderful fruit-forward and award-winning wines come from this area, where volcanic ash is in some of the soil and many of the vineyards are located at high altitudes. The grapes here include Cabernet Sauvignon, Merlot, Syrah, Chardonnay, Sauvignon Blanc, and Muscat.

2. <u>JUDEAN HILLS:</u> Many of the vineyards are terraced on steep hills, which create more of an earthy style of wine with a deeper minerality.

3. <u>SAMSON (SHIMSON) REGION:</u> This is the country's second largest wine grape region on the central coastal plain.

4. <u>NEGEV REGION:</u> This is a semi-arid area that relies on irrigation and contains coarse, gravelly soil.

5. <u>SHAMRON:</u> This is Israel's largest wine grape growing region and contains chalky soil. A variety of grapes are grown here.

There are many wonderful vineyards and wineries in Israel. Here are a few of them:

<u>BINYAMINA WINE CELLARS:</u> This winery produces wine from a variety of grapes, including Cabernet Sauvignon, Chardonnay, Merlot, Sauvignon Blanc, Shiraz, Tempranillo, Zinfandel, and Gewurztraminer.

<u>CARMEL WINERIES:</u> This is a very historic winery. At the time of this writing, over 65 percent of all of the wine grapes grown in Israel are processed in their facilities.

<u>GOLAN HEIGHTS WINERY:</u> This is one of the largest wineries in Israel and produces a wide range of wines

<u>BEN AMI:</u> This winery produces a Cabernet Sauvignon, a Chardonnay, and a Merlot that is consistently good.

<u>BARKAN:</u> This winery creates wonderful wines from many grapes, including, among others, Petit Syrah, Pinotage, Pinot Noir, and Muscat.

Here are just a few of the many international producers/wines: **Herzog Wine Cellars** in California; **Red Fern Cellars** in New York; **Hagafen** in Napa; **Beckett's Flat** in Australia; New Zealand's **Goose Bay** and **Teal Lake**; **Alfasi** in Chile; **Bartenura, Abarbanel,** and **Rashi** in Italy; **Ramon Cardova** in Spain; **Bodegas Flechas de los Andes** in Argentina; **Blacksberg** in South Africa; **Baron Rothschild Haut-Medoc; Barrail de Zede Bordeaux Superieur; Ch. Labegorce Zede Margaux;** plus estates in Chablis, Rhone, Vin de Pays, and even Champagnes. **The Covenant** wine, California…sublime!

CHAPTER FIVE

Shopping for Kosher Wine – Things to Consider

"I will grant you the rain of your land in its due season, the first rain and the latter rain, that you may gather in your new grain and your wine and your oil."
—Deuteronomy 11:14

It is important that wine be treated properly all the way from the winery to the distributor (who stores and ships the wine) to the retailer (who stores and displays the wine) to you (who brings the wine home). Approximately 5 percent of bottles of wine using standard cork closures become spoiled and undrinkable due to faulty corks. A number of wines also go bad because of improper handling somewhere along the line. Thankfully, there are safeguards that can be used to lessen the chance of getting a bad bottle.

You may be lucky enough to live in an area with a great kosher market featuring many wines and wine tastings. If so, that's great! If not, don't despair. Find a reputable wine store with knowledgeable sales people. Many general wine merchants carry some kosher wines, but they haven't necessarily tried any of them. For this reason, it may be difficult to get a personal recommendation about kosher wines. Ask the merchant if he or she will open a bottle for you to sample. They might oblige you. If they seem hesitant, perhaps they would be willing to open up a bottle to sample if you brought in a few friends who might also purchase some wine. Doing this would be informative and lots of fun.

To prevent the corks from drying out, bottles should ideally be displayed on their sides at the store. This allows the corks to remain in contact with the wine. A dry cork allows too much air into the bottle. This could cause the wine to oxidize, which could negatively alter its flavor. Of course, bottles with screw caps don't need to be stored this way. Don't hesitate to purchase wine that has a screw cap instead of a cork. They offer excellent protection by not allowing any air into the bottle, thereby preventing oxidation. This is particularly beneficial for young wines that should be consumed without any additional aging. This is most often the style of wine you will find in bottles with screw caps or corks. The temperature is also important. Heat and light are the enemies of wine. The store should not be too warm and the wines should not be exposed to direct sunlight through the windows. Expensive, high-end wines should be stored in temperature-controlled units.

Getting your wine home from the store

In taking your wine home, the objective is to not allow the wine to cook by being kept in a hot car for an extended period of time. If you can't get home for more than a few hours, you can store the wine in a Styrofoam container for protection. Another option is to buy the wine on your way home!

Some Kosher Symbols to Look For

There are many kosher certification organizations around the world. They employ any number of symbols to signify the kosher status of the wine. Here are just a few examples you will find on bottles of kosher wine. You can go online to research this even further.

CHAPTER SIX

Storing and Serving Wines at Home

"It shall come to pass in that day that mountains shall drip sweet wine and the hills shall flow with milk."
–Joel 3:18

Kosher or otherwise, the vast majority of wines made nowadays are designed to be consumed within a short period of time after they have been purchased. We buy the wine at a local market, bring it home, and enjoy a glass or two that very day or within a couple of weeks. Sometimes, though, we may earmark our bottle for some future occasion. We may want to hold this special wine for a few weeks, many months, or even years. We might also want to make a large purchase and stock up when there is a good sale. Whether we drink the wine immediately or hold off until later, the quality and integrity of all wine should be preserved.

WHITES

Ideally, white wines should be stored in a wine cooler at a stable temperature between 55 and 60 degrees Fahrenheit (12.8 and

15.6 degrees Celsius). If they will be consumed within four or five days, most white wines can be stored directly in the refrigerator. Refrigerators have the added benefit of maintaining a good serving temperature. If there is room, place the bottles on their sides to keep the cork moist. After more than four or five days, the refrigerator may be too cold. If there is no other way to keep the wine as cold as it would be in a refrigerator, put the wine in a cool, dark closet or cupboard. It should ideally be placed somewhere where there is no direct sunlight and the temperature will not fluctuate very much, if at all. It is fine to store an average wine for a few weeks or months in a wine rack that is stored away from direct sunlight and heat from TVs, dishwashers, and stoves. Pop the wine in the fridge several hours before you want to open it. It must be mentioned that—with a few exceptions—white wines are not meant to be aged. A bottle of white wine is ready to drink the moment you purchase it. However, some white Burgundy wines, high-end German Rieslings, and certain high-end sweet dessert wines do benefit from additional aging.

The proper serving temperature for white wines is between 48 and 58 degrees Fahrenheit (8.88 to 14.44 degrees Celsius). High-end, fine white wines need to be served at the higher end of this temperature range. These exceptionally well-crafted wines have more complex flavors and nuances—hence the higher price—that would not be apparent if the wine were too cold. The lack of quality in white wines of lesser value can be disguised by serving it colder. Take a white wine that has been stored at room temperature and place it in the refrigerator for at least two to three hours to get it nicely chilled. Keep a wine bucket with ice in it to help maintain the temperature of the wine.

REDS

Ideally, red wines are stored at 55 degrees Fahrenheit (12.77 degrees Celsius) and placed on their sides to allow the wine contact with the cork. As with white wines, in the absence of a wine cellar or wine cooler, many people store their red wines in racks on a counter or in non-temperature controlled cabinets. This is perfectly acceptable for the short-term (several weeks or a few months) storage of a few bottles, as long as the bottles are not exposed to direct sunlight through a window or placed close to the oven or another heat source. You would not, for example, want to store your wine on the countertop above the dishwasher or beside your TV. For larger quantities of wine (a case or more) that you plan to hold for a year or longer, you can use a dark, cool closet or a cupboard where the temperature does not fluctuate. For very fine red wines that should be held for a number of years, you should invest in a temperature-controlled wine cabinet. The necessity of doing this cannot be overstated. The environment greatly influences the characteristics of finer wines as they mature over the years. Proper temperature and humidity makes all of the difference. If space is limited and you are lucky enough to have acquired some fine, age-worthy wines, a little research should lead you to some merchants who offer quality in-store wine storage.

Lighter-bodied red wines like certain Sangioveses, Merlots, and Pinot Noirs are at their best when they are served around 58 degrees Fahrenheit (14.44 degrees Celsius). Full-bodied, rich, big red wines like Cabernet Sauvignons, robust Italian wines, and fine Bordeaux are at their best when they are served around 65 degrees Fahrenheit (18.33 degrees Celsius). Red wines are often served too warm—at so-called room temperature. This historic expression is no longer valid. Keep in mind that rooms in today's homes can range from 70 degrees Fahrenheit (21.11 degrees Celsius) to 80 degrees Fahrenheit (26.66 degrees Celsius) or more. This is too warm to be an appropriate serving temperature. When served too warm, a wine can taste flat and it won't show off its balance between alcohol, fruit, and tannins. To bring a red wine that is stored at room temperature to a proper serving temperature, place the bottle in the refrigerator for about fifteen minutes before serving. This slight chill really brings out the wonderful fruit in any red wine!

ROSÉ

Many of the same considerations that apply to white wines also apply to rosé wines. For a sweeter taste, serve them around 48 degrees Fahrenheit (8.88 degrees Celsius), for a drier—and usually more complex—taste, serve them around 58 degrees Fahrenheit (14.44 degrees Celsius).

SPARKLING
WINES AND CHAMPAGNES

As with white wines, you should store sparkling wines and Champagnes between 55 and 60 degrees Fahrenheit (12.77 degrees C. to 15.55 degrees Celsius), but you should serve them at the much colder, ideal temperature of around 42 degrees Fahrenheit (5.55 degrees Celsius). By the way, that loud pop of the cork when you open the bottle is not, as commonly thought, a good thing. It is an indication that the champagne is not cold enough.

CHAPTER SEVEN

Pairing Wine with Food: General Guidelines

"He causes grass to sprout for the animals and vegetation for the work of man, to bring forth bread from the earth. And wine, which cheers man's heart, to make the face shine from oil, and bread, which sustains man's heart."
–Psalms 104:14-15

Many people feel confused when trying to select the right wine—kosher or otherwise—to have with their meal. It can be seen as a formidable task that is beyond the scope of the average consumer. There are so many options: red, white, rosé, sparkling, sweet, dry, fruity, or earthy. The fact is, however, that it is easier than ever to get a delicious bottle of kosher wine to complement your special meal and please all of your family members and guests.

You have likely heard of certain rules for matching wine with food. White wine goes with fish and red wine goes with meat. Light style wines should be served before bold ones wines and dry wines should be served before sweet wines. These should be considered guidelines than rules, but the advice is still sound. Do you know why this is the case? We simply don't want wine to be so bold and flavorful that it overpowers the taste of food. We also don't want wine that is so light-bodied that its aromas and taste seem to disappear when consumed with a heavy meal. It makes sense that big (higher alcohol content) and full-bodied (rich, dark fruit flavors with a lingering finish), oaky, red wines with strong tannins (an astringent element derived from the skins, pits, and stems of the grapes and from oak barrels during fermentation) such as Cabernet Sauvignon might not be appropriate to have with a mild white fish prepared in a delicate cream sauce. But if you serve that red wine with your juicy Shabbat brisket or herb-roasted chicken, they will complement and highlight each other's flavors beautifully! The proteins and the fat in the brisket and chicken harmonize with the tannins in the wine, creating a smooth partnership and a delicious combination.

It's important to note that the actual color of the wine (i.e., red versus white) is not the most important aspect in pairing wine with food. There are lighter-bodied, smooth reds with very little tannins that work very well with fish. Pairing a Pinot Noir with broiled salmon is a classic example. It would not be difficult to find a rich, full-bodied Chardonnay that could easily hold its own with a heavy meat dish. To ensure a successful pairing, we look for a good balance between the flavors and richness of the meal and the weight (alcohol levels, acidity, oak influences, etc.) of the wine. **Here's the big secret: Ultimately, any wine you personally enjoy with your food creates a successful pairing!**

LOWER ALCOHOL WINES

It is worth mentioning that there are many kosher wines with lower alcohol levels. Usually, most wines have between 12 and 15 percent alcohol by volume, and this is always noted on the label. Lower alcohol wines can be as low as 4 percent, which is a considerable difference. The lower alcohol wines generally vary from a little sweet to very sweet, and most of the time they are light-bodied. They are wonderful to have at holidays during which many glasses of wine are customarily poured. Think of the Passover Seder and its four-glass requirement. Senior family members and guests might also appreciate having less alcohol in their wine. Remember, the bottle's label will display the alcohol content.

Bartenura, a winery from Italy, has a line of low-alcohol wines, including white Moscato and a red Malvasia.

Here is an example of an alcohol-by-volume note that you will find on your bottle:

ALC. BY VOL. 9.2%

NET CONT.: 750ml

CHAPTER EIGHT

Traditional Holiday
Food and Wine Pairing

"Eat the bread with Joy and drink the wine with a merry heart."
–Ecclesiastes 9:7

Here are some traditional holiday menus with wine suggestions. If you cannot locate these particular wines, simply substitute the same wine style from another kosher producer. ***Please note that a number of these wine producers create kosher AND non-kosher wines, so you must check the bottles for the appropriate kosher symbols.*** And remember, ultimately any wine you personally enjoy with your food creates a wonderful match!

THE WEEKLY SHABBAT MEAL

MENU #1

Challah bread

Vegetable soup

Garlic roast chicken

Herb roasted potatoes

Steamed green beans

THE WINES:

WHITES: Chardonnay, medium-bodied to fuller-bodied Pinot Grigio or Pinot Gris, or Chenin Blanc.

S'Forno Pinot Grigio Veneto / Baron Herzog Chenin Blanc, Clarksville, California / Yarden Chardonnay

REDS: Medium-bodied and full-bodied Pinot Noirs; Merlots, light-medium Bordeaux

Hagafen Merlot, Napa / Goosebay Pinot Noir, Marlborough, New Zealand / Ch La Tour Seran, Cru Bourgeois, Medoc

THE WEEKLY SHABBAT MEAL

MENU #2

Challah bread

Mixed green salad with fruited vinaigrette

Beef cholent

THE WINES

WHITES: Off-dry Riesling, medium bodied Chardonnay, or Gewürztraminer.

Hagafen White Riesling, Napa / Ben Ami Chardonnay, Galilee / Carmel Gewurztraminer, Upper Galilee

REDS: Rhone-style reds, Italian Chianti Classicos, Spanish Tempranillo-based blends

Chateau Ministre Coteaux Grenache-Syrah blend, Languedoc / Bartenura Chianti, Italy / Bodegas Casa Quemada, Tempranillo / Castilla, Spain

ROSHASHANA

MENU #1

Round challah bread

Gefilte fish with grated horseradish

Chicken soup

Sweet brisket with carrots & potato

THE WINES

WHITES: Sparkling wine, medium-full-bodied oaked Chardonnay, or full-bodied dry blends.

NV Laurent-Perrier Cuvee Rose Brut, France / Yarden Chardonnay, Israel / White Wine, Welnerberg, South Africa

REDS: medium-bodied super-Tuscan wine, Cabernet, blends

Giordano Borgo Real Toscano, Rosso, Italy / Segal's Cabernet Special Res, Israel / Ch Le Breuil Renaissance, France

ROSHASHANA

Menu #2

Round challah bread

A salad of cucumbers, tomatoes, and bib lettuce

Baked apricot chicken

Mashed potato and onion

Seasoned green beans

The Wines

WHITES: Moscato D'Asti , Viognier, or Chenin Blanc.

Bartenura Moscato, Italy / Carmel Appellation Series, Viognier, Israel / Baron Herzog Chenin Blanc, U.S.A.

REDS: New-World style Pinot Noirs, fruit driven Merlots; fruit forward Shiraz

Goose Bay Pinot Noir, New Zealand / Alfasi Merlot, Chile / Teal Lake Shiraz, Australia

YOM KIPPUR

Menu #1

Dairy breakfast and brunch

Egg soufflés

Blintzes

Cottage cheese or cream cheese

Kugel

Fresh fruit salad

The Wines

WHITES: Lower-alcohol sparkling wines and off-dry white wines

Bartenura Moscato D'Asti, Italy / Abarbanel Gewurztraminer, Alsace

YOM KIPPUR

MENU #2

Smoked salmon and smoked carp

Whitefish salad and herring salad

Sliced tomatoes and onions

Assorted bagels

THE WINES

WHITES: Sparkling wines or off-dry white wines

Carmel Young Carignano, Israel / Tierra Salvaje Cava Brut Res., Spain / Herzog Vouvray, U.S.A

HANUKAH

MENU #1

Butternut Squash Soup

Chicken Schnitzel

Couscous

Herbed green beans

THE WINES

WHITES (entrée): Medium-bodied white wine or brut sparkling wine.

Tierra Salvaje Sauvignon Blanc, Maule Valley, Chile / Ben Ami Chardonnay, Israel / Pommery Brut Champagne, France

REDS (entrée): Medium-bodied Cabernet Sauvignon or Merlot.

Benyamina, Tiltan N.V., Israel; Herzog Merlot Special Reserve, Alexander Valley, U.S.A.

HANUKAH

MENU #2

Mixed Green Salad

Broiled Salmon

Potato Latkes, Applesauce, Sour Cream

Sautéed Broccoli

THE WINES

WHITES (entrée): Sauvignon Blanc, Fume Blanc, or Oaked Chardonnay.

Goosebay Sauvignon Blanc, Marlborough, New Zealand / Goosebay Chardonnay, Marlborough, New Zealand

REDS (entrée): Pinot Noir or medium-bodied Rioja

Hagafen Pinot Noir Napa, U.S.A. / Elvi, Matiz Rioja, Spain

PASSOVER

MENU #1

Matzah

Haroset

Chicken soup with matzah balls

Stuffed breast of veal

Boiled new potatoes with dill

Green beans

THE WINES

WHITES (entrée): Medium-bodied to full-bodied Chardonnay, or Viognier

Yardem Chardonnay Odem Organic, Israel / Yatir Viognier, U.S.A.

REDS (entrée): Malbec or Bordeaux.

Bodegas Flechas de Los Andes, Argentina / Barons Edmund & Benjamin De Rothschild, Haut Medoc, France

PASSOVER

Menu #2

Matzah

Haroset

Gefilte fish

Garlic lamb

Roasted potatoes and carrots and onions

The Wines

WHITES (entrée): Fuller-bodied Chardonnay.

Hagafen Chardonnay Oak Knoll, Napa, California / Herzog Chardonnay Special Reserve Russian River Valley, California

REDS: Cabernet Sauvignon blends or Syrah

Beckett's Flat Cabernet Sauvignon-Shiraz, Margaret River, Western Australia / Four Gates Syrah, Santa Cruz Mountains, California

SHAVUOT

MENU #1

Mushroom barley soup

Crisp mixed greens with herb dressing

Broiled grouper

Rice with mixed vegetables

THE WINES

WHITES: Fuller-bodied Sauvignon Blanc or richer blends.

Gamla Sauvignon Blanc, Israel / Herzog Selection Chateneuf White Bordeaux

REDS: Pinot Noirs, medium-bodied red Zinfandels

Teal Lake Pinot Noir, Australia / Baron Herzog Zinfandel, U.S.A.

SHAVUOT

MENU #2

Vegetable soup

Green salad

Eggplant Parmesan

THE WINES

WHITES: Pinot Grigio or Soave.

Bartenura Pinot Grigio, Italy/ Bartenura Soave, Italy

REDS: Chianti or Nebbiolo.

Bartenura Chianti / Bartenura Langhe Nebbiolo, Italy

PURIM

MENU #1

Vegetable broth

Roast asparagus

Sautéed mushrooms

Israeli salad

Vegetable kugel

THE WINES

REDS: Earthy and fruity red wines.

Cantina Borgo Real Primativo, Italy / Ramon Cordova Rioja

WHITES: medium-bodied to full-bodied.

Goosebay Sauvignon Blanc, Marlborough, New Zealand / Domaine Ducastel "C" Chardonnay Blanc du Castel, Israel

PURIM

Menu #2

Chicken soup with Kreplach

Steamed whole fish with white wine and herbs

Broccoli with olives

White rice

The Wines

WHITE: Similar to wine that is used to cook fish. Medium-bodied to fuller-bodied Sauvignon Blanc or unoaked Chardonnay.

Pascal Bouchard Chablis, France / Tierre Salvaje Sauvignon Blanc, Chile

RED: Light-bodied to medium-bodied, lower tannin red wine.

Ben Ami Merlot, Israel / Gabriele Chianti, Italy

SUKKOT

MENU

Vegetable soup

Sweet and sour tongue

Roasted root vegetables

Couscous

THE WINES

REDS: medium-bodied Douro or fuller-bodied Petit Syrah.

Herzog Petit Syrah Limited Edition, Lodi, U.S.A. / Casa Da Corca Reserva, Douro, Portugal

WHITES: full-bodied dry wines or off-dry white wines.

Goosebay Chardonnay, Marlborough, New Zealand / Hagafen Chardonnay Prix Reserve Oak Knoll, U.S.A.

CHAPTER NINE

Your Holiday Wine Journal

"The earth shall respond to the corn, the wine, and the oil."
—Hosea 2:24

Keep some helpful notes on kosher wines that you have had at holiday meals. What wines were they? What food did you have with them? Was it a good pairing? What kind of impression did the wine leave with you and your family and guests? These notes can assist you with future wine purchases.

THE OCCASION AND SOME NOTES:

HOLIDAY AND MENU

Date   *Wine (Name, Winemaker, Region, Year)* *Cost*
         Mevushal?

THE OCCASION AND SOME NOTES:

Holiday and Menu

Date	Wine (Name, Winemaker, Region, Year) Mevushal?	Cost

THE OCCASION AND SOME NOTES:

HOLIDAY AND MENU

Date	Wine (Name, Winemaker, Region, Year) Mevushal?	Cost

THE OCCASION AND SOME NOTES:

Holiday and Menu

Date	Wine (Name, Winemaker, Region, Year) Mevushal?	Cost

THE OCCASION AND SOME NOTES:

HOLIDAY AND MENU

Date	Wine (Name, Winemaker, Region, Year) Mevushal?	Cost

THE OCCASION AND SOME NOTES:

Holiday and Menu

Date	Wine (Name, Winemaker, Region, Year) Mevushal?	Cost

THE OCCASION AND SOME NOTES:

HOLIDAY AND MENU

Date	Wine (Name, Winemaker, Region, Year) Mevushal?	Cost

THE OCCASION AND SOME NOTES:

Holiday and Menu

Date	Wine (Name, Winemaker, Region, Year) Mevushal?	Cost

THE OCCASION AND SOME NOTES:

Holiday and Menu

Date   *Wine (Name, Winemaker, Region, Year)*   *Cost*
Mevushal?

THE OCCASION AND SOME NOTES:

HOLIDAY AND MENU

Date   Wine (Name, Winemaker, Region, Year)   Cost
                        Mevushal?

THE OCCASION AND SOME NOTES:

HOLIDAY AND MENU

Date	Wine (Name, Winemaker, Region, Year) Mevushal?	Cost

THE OCCASION AND SOME NOTES:

HOLIDAY AND MENU

Date   *Wine (Name, Winemaker, Region, Year)*   *Cost*
                          Mevushal?

THE OCCASION AND SOME NOTES:

Holiday and Menu

Date	Wine (Name, Winemaker, Region, Year) Mevushal?	Cost

THE OCCASION AND SOME NOTES:

Holiday and Menu

Date	Wine (Name, Winemaker, Region, Year) Mevushal?	Cost

THE OCCASION AND SOME NOTES:

HOLIDAY AND MENU

Date *Wine (Name, Winemaker, Region, Year)* *Cost*
Mevushal?

THE OCCASION AND SOME NOTES:

Holiday and Menu

Date	Wine (Name, Winemaker, Region, Year) Mevushal?	Cost

THE OCCASION AND SOME NOTES:

HOLIDAY AND MENU

Date	Wine (Name, Winemaker, Region, Year) Mevushal?	Cost

THE OCCASION AND SOME NOTES:

Holiday and Menu

Date	Wine (Name, Winemaker, Region, Year) Mevushal?	Cost

THE OCCASION AND SOME NOTES:

HOLIDAY AND MENU

Date	Wine (Name, Winemaker, Region, Year) Mevushal?	Cost

THE OCCASION AND SOME NOTES:

Holiday and Menu

Date	Wine (Name, Winemaker, Region, Year) Mevushal?	Cost

THE OCCASION AND SOME NOTES:

Holiday and Menu

Date	Wine (Name, Winemaker, Region, Year) Mevushal?	Cost

THE OCCASION AND SOME NOTES:

Holiday and Menu

Date	Wine (Name, Winemaker, Region, Year) Mevushal?	Cost

THE OCCASION AND SOME NOTES:

HOLIDAY AND MENU

Date　　　　*Wine (Name, Winemaker, Region, Year)*　　　*Cost*
　　　　　　　　　　　　Mevushal?

THE OCCASION AND SOME NOTES:

HOLIDAY AND MENU

Date   *Wine (Name, Winemaker, Region, Year)*   *Cost*
                Mevushal?

THE OCCASION AND SOME NOTES:

HOLIDAY AND MENU

Date	Wine (Name, Winemaker, Region, Year) Mevushal?	Cost

THE OCCASION AND SOME NOTES:

Holiday and Menu

Date	Wine (Name, Winemaker, Region, Year) Mevushal?	Cost

THE OCCASION AND SOME NOTES:

HOLIDAY AND MENU

Date	Wine (Name, Winemaker, Region, Year) Mevushal?	Cost

THE OCCASION AND SOME NOTES:

HOLIDAY AND MENU

Date	Wine (Name, Winemaker, Region, Year) Mevushal?	Cost

THE OCCASION AND SOME NOTES:

HOLIDAY AND MENU

Date	Wine (Name, Winemaker, Region, Year) Mevushal?	Cost

THE OCCASION AND SOME NOTES:

HOLIDAY AND MENU

Date	Wine (Name, Winemaker, Region, Year) Mevushal?	Cost

THE OCCASION AND SOME NOTES:

HOLIDAY AND MENU

Date	Wine (Name, Winemaker, Region, Year) Mevushal?	Cost

THE OCCASION AND SOME NOTES:

HOLIDAY AND MENU

Date   *Wine (Name, Winemaker, Region, Year)*   *Cost*
Mevushal?

THE OCCASION AND SOME NOTES:

HOLIDAY AND MENU

Date	Wine (Name, Winemaker, Region, Year) Mevushal?	Cost

THE OCCASION AND SOME NOTES:

Holiday and Menu

Date	Wine (Name, Winemaker, Region, Year) Mevushal?	Cost

THE OCCASION AND SOME NOTES:

HOLIDAY AND MENU

Date   Wine (Name, Winemaker, Region, Year)   Cost
                              Mevushal?

THE OCCASION AND SOME NOTES:

Holiday and Menu

Date	Wine (Name, Winemaker, Region, Year) Mevushal?	Cost

THE OCCASION AND SOME NOTES:

HOLIDAY AND MENU

Date	Wine (Name, Winemaker, Region, Year) Mevushal?	Cost

THE OCCASION AND SOME NOTES:

Holiday and Menu

Date	Wine (Name, Winemaker, Region, Year) Mevushal?	Cost

THE OCCASION AND SOME NOTES:

HOLIDAY AND MENU

Date   *Wine (Name, Winemaker, Region, Year)*   *Cost*
Mevushal?

THE OCCASION AND SOME NOTES:

Holiday and Menu

Date	Wine (Name, Winemaker, Region, Year)	Cost
	Mevushal?	

THE OCCASION AND SOME NOTES:

HOLIDAY AND MENU

Date	Wine (Name, Winemaker, Region, Year) Mevushal?	Cost

THE OCCASION AND SOME NOTES:

Holiday and Menu

Date	Wine (Name, Winemaker, Region, Year) Mevushal?	Cost

THE OCCASION AND SOME NOTES:

HOLIDAY AND MENU

Date	Wine (Name, Winemaker, Region, Year) Mevushal?	Cost

THE OCCASION AND SOME NOTES:

HOLIDAY AND MENU

Date	Wine (Name, Winemaker, Region, Year) Mevushal?	Cost

THE OCCASION AND SOME NOTES:

Holiday and Menu

Date	Wine (Name, Winemaker, Region, Year) Mevushal?	Cost

THE OCCASION AND SOME NOTES:

Holiday and Menu

Date	Wine (Name, Winemaker, Region, Year) Mevushal?	Cost

THE OCCASION AND SOME NOTES:

HOLIDAY AND MENU

Date	Wine (Name, Winemaker, Region, Year) Mevushal?	Cost

THE OCCASION AND SOME NOTES:

HOLIDAY AND MENU

Date	Wine (Name, Winemaker, Region, Year) Mevushal?	Cost

THE OCCASION AND SOME NOTES:

HOLIDAY AND MENU

Date	Wine (Name, Winemaker, Region, Year) Mevushal?	Cost

THE OCCASION AND SOME NOTES:

HOLIDAY AND MENU

Date	*Wine (Name, Winemaker, Region, Year)* *Mevushal?*	*Cost*

THE OCCASION AND SOME NOTES:

HOLIDAY AND MENU

Date	Wine (Name, Winemaker, Region, Year) Mevushal?	Cost

THE OCCASION AND SOME NOTES:

HOLIDAY AND MENU

Date	Wine (Name, Winemaker, Region, Year) Mevushal?	Cost

THE OCCASION AND SOME NOTES:

HOLIDAY AND MENU

Date	Wine (Name, Winemaker, Region, Year) Mevushal?	Cost

THE OCCASION AND SOME NOTES:

Holiday and Menu

Date	Wine (Name, Winemaker, Region, Year) Mevushal?	Cost

THE OCCASION AND SOME NOTES:

HOLIDAY AND MENU

Date	Wine (Name, Winemaker, Region, Year) Mevushal?	Cost

THE OCCASION AND SOME NOTES:

Holiday and Menu

Date   *Wine (Name, Winemaker, Region, Year)*   *Cost*
                         Mevushal?

THE OCCASION AND SOME NOTES:

HOLIDAY AND MENU

Date	Wine (Name, Winemaker, Region, Year) Mevushal?	Cost

THE OCCASION AND SOME NOTES:

HOLIDAY AND MENU

Date	Wine (Name, Winemaker, Region, Year) Mevushal?	Cost

THE OCCASION AND SOME NOTES:

HOLIDAY AND MENU

Date	Wine (Name, Winemaker, Region, Year) Mevushal?	Cost

THE OCCASION AND SOME NOTES:

HOLIDAY AND MENU

Date	Wine (Name, Winemaker, Region, Year) Mevushal?	Cost

THE OCCASION AND SOME NOTES:

Holiday and Menu

Date	Wine (Name, Winemaker, Region, Year) Mevushal?	Cost

THE OCCASION AND SOME NOTES:

Holiday and Menu

Date	Wine (Name, Winemaker, Region, Year) Mevushal?	Cost

THE OCCASION AND SOME NOTES:

HOLIDAY AND MENU

Date	Wine (Name, Winemaker, Region, Year) Mevushal?	Cost

THE OCCASION AND SOME NOTES:

HOLIDAY AND MENU

Date	Wine (Name, Winemaker, Region, Year) Mevushal?	Cost

THE OCCASION AND SOME NOTES:

Holiday and Menu

Date	Wine (Name, Winemaker, Region, Year) Mevushal?	Cost

THE OCCASION AND SOME NOTES:

Holiday and Menu

Date	Wine (Name, Winemaker, Region, Year) Mevushal?	Cost

THE OCCASION AND SOME NOTES:

HOLIDAY AND MENU

Date   *Wine (Name, Winemaker, Region, Year)*   *Cost*
                  Mevushal?

THE OCCASION AND SOME NOTES:

Holiday and Menu

Date	Wine (Name, Winemaker, Region, Year) Mevushal?	Cost

THE OCCASION AND SOME NOTES:

HOLIDAY AND MENU

Date	Wine (Name, Winemaker, Region, Year) Mevushal?	Cost

THE OCCASION AND SOME NOTES:

Holiday and Menu

Date	Wine (Name, Winemaker, Region, Year) Mevushal?	Cost

THE OCCASION AND SOME NOTES:

Holiday and Menu

Date	Wine (Name, Winemaker, Region, Year) Mevushal?	Cost

THE OCCASION AND SOME NOTES:

Holiday and Menu

Date	Wine (Name, Winemaker, Region, Year) Mevushal?	Cost

THE OCCASION AND SOME NOTES:

HOLIDAY AND MENU

Date	Wine (Name, Winemaker, Region, Year) Mevushal?	Cost

THE OCCASION AND SOME NOTES:

Holiday and Menu

Date   *Wine (Name, Winemaker, Region, Year)*   *Cost*
                            Mevushal?

THE OCCASION AND SOME NOTES:

HOLIDAY AND MENU

Date	Wine (Name, Winemaker, Region, Year) Mevushal?	Cost

THE OCCASION AND SOME NOTES:

HOLIDAY AND MENU

Date	Wine (Name, Winemaker, Region, Year) Mevushal?	Cost

THE OCCASION AND SOME NOTES:

HOLIDAY AND MENU

Date	Wine (Name, Winemaker, Region, Year) Mevushal?	Cost

THE OCCASION AND SOME NOTES:

HOLIDAY AND MENU

Date   *Wine (Name, Winemaker, Region, Year)*   *Cost*
                                    Mevushal?

THE OCCASION AND SOME NOTES:

HOLIDAY AND MENU

Date   *Wine (Name, Winemaker, Region, Year)*   *Cost*
                        Mevushal?

THE OCCASION AND SOME NOTES:

HOLIDAY AND MENU

Date   *Wine (Name, Winemaker, Region, Year)*   *Cost*
                          Mevushal?

THE OCCASION AND SOME NOTES:

HOLIDAY AND MENU

Date	Wine (Name, Winemaker, Region, Year) Mevushal?	Cost

THE OCCASION AND SOME NOTES:

Holiday and Menu

Date	Wine (Name, Winemaker, Region, Year) Mevushal?	Cost

THE OCCASION AND SOME NOTES:

HOLIDAY AND MENU

Date	Wine (Name, Winemaker, Region, Year) Mevushal?	Cost

THE OCCASION AND SOME NOTES:

Holiday and Menu

Date	Wine (Name, Winemaker, Region, Year) Mevushal?	Cost

THE OCCASION AND SOME NOTES:

HOLIDAY AND MENU

Date	Wine (Name, Winemaker, Region, Year) Mevushal?	Cost

THE OCCASION AND SOME NOTES:

HOLIDAY AND MENU

Date   *Wine (Name, Winemaker, Region, Year)*   *Cost*
Mevushal?

THE OCCASION AND SOME NOTES:

HOLIDAY AND MENU

Date	Wine (Name, Winemaker, Region, Year) Mevushal?	Cost

THE OCCASION AND SOME NOTES:

HOLIDAY AND MENU

Date	Wine (Name, Winemaker, Region, Year) Mevushal?	Cost

THE OCCASION AND SOME NOTES:

Holiday and Menu

Date	Wine (Name, Winemaker, Region, Year) Mevushal?	Cost

THE OCCASION AND SOME NOTES:

HOLIDAY AND MENU

Date	Wine (Name, Winemaker, Region, Year) Mevushal?	Cost

THE OCCASION AND SOME NOTES:

HOLIDAY AND MENU

Date	Wine (Name, Winemaker, Region, Year) Mevushal?	Cost

THE OCCASION AND SOME NOTES:

Holiday and Menu

Date	Wine (Name, Winemaker, Region, Year) Mevushal?	Cost

THE OCCASION AND SOME NOTES:

HOLIDAY AND MENU

Date	Wine (Name, Winemaker, Region, Year) Mevushal?	Cost

THE OCCASION AND SOME NOTES:

HOLIDAY AND MENU

Date	Wine (Name, Winemaker, Region, Year) Mevushal?	Cost

THE OCCASION AND SOME NOTES:

HOLIDAY AND MENU

Date	Wine (Name, Winemaker, Region, Year) Mevushal?	Cost

THE OCCASION AND SOME NOTES:

Holiday and Menu

Date   *Wine (Name, Winemaker, Region, Year)*   *Cost*
                              Mevushal?

THE OCCASION AND SOME NOTES:

HOLIDAY AND MENU

Date	Wine (Name, Winemaker, Region, Year) Mevushal?	Cost

There are many, many wonderful books, articles, videos, websites, and articles about all things related to wine! Here are some I highly recommend

BIBLIOGRAPHY

Dornenburg, Andrew and Page, Karen. *What to Drink with What You Eat*. New York: Bulfinch Press, 2006.

Fellner, Judith B. *In the Jewish Tradition: A Year of Food and Festivities*. New York: Smithmark Publishers, Inc., 1995.

Glazer, Phyllis with Glazer, Miriyam. *The Essential Book of Jewish Festival Cooking*. New York: HarperCollins Publishers, 2004.

Harpur, Tom. *The Spirituality of Wine*. Kelowna, British Columbia: Northstone Publishing, 2004.

Henderson, J. Patrick and Rex, Dellie. *About Wine*. Cliff Park, NY: Thomson Delmar Learning, 2007.

Herbst, Ron and Sharon Tyler. *The New Wine Lover's Companion*. New York: Barron's Educational Series, Inc., 2003.

Immer, Andrea. *Great Tastes Made Simple*. New York: Broadway Books, 2002.

McCarthy, Ed and Ewing-Mulligan, Mary. *Wine for Dummies: 4*[th] *Edition*. Hoboken, NJ: Wiley Publishing, Inc. 2006.

McNutt, Joni G. *In Praise of Wine*. Santa Barbara, CA: Capra Press, 1993.

Nathan, Joan. *Joan Nathan's Jewish Holiday Cookbook*. New York: Schocken Books, 2004.

Olitzky, Rabbi Kerry M. and Judson, Rabbi Daniel. *Jewish Holidays: A Brief Introduction for Christians*. Woodstock, VT: Jewish Lights Publishing, 2007.

Rosengarten, David and Wesson, Joshua. *Red Wine with Fish: The New Art of Matching Wine with Food.* New York: Simon and Schuster, 1989.

Smith, Brian H. *The Sommelier's Guide to Wine.* New York: Black Dog and Leventhal Publishers, 2003.

Smith, Jeff, *The Frugal Gourmet Cooks with Wine.* New York: William Morrow and Company, 1989.

HTTP://KOSHERFOOD.ABOUT.COM

WWW.GOISRAEL.COM

HTTP://ROYALWINE.COM

Made in the USA
Columbia, SC
05 April 2018